Notting Hill Editions

Notting Hill Editions is an independent British Publisher
devoted to reviving the art of the essay. The company was founded
by Tom Kremer, champion of innovation and the man responsible
for popularising the Rubik's Cube.

After a successful business career in toy invention, Tom decided,
at the age of eighty, to engage his life-long passion for the essay. In a
digital world, where time is short and books are cheap, he judged the
moment was right to launch a counter-culture. He founded Notting
Hill Editions with a mission: to restore this largely neglected art as
a cornerstone of literary culture, and to produce beautiful books
that would not be thrown away.

The unique purpose of the essay is to try out ideas and see where
they lead. Hailed as 'the shape of things to come' we aim to publish
books that shift perspectives, prompt argument, make imaginative
leaps and reveal truth. In short, books that grow their readers.

To discover more, please visit
www.nottinghilleditions.com

*'Nothing is lost. That's why writers write.*
*Or maybe everything is lost, and that's why they write.*
*Nostalgia has both bases covered: the doneness*
*of things, and the ongoingness of things, and it*
*is between the doneness and the ongoingness*
*that the inside of our lives takes place.'*

Patrick McGuinness, 'The Future of Nostalgia'

*'I remember that life was just as serious then as it is now.'*

Joe Brainard, *I Remember*

*'All children talk to their toys;
the toys become actors in the great
drama of life, scaled down inside the
camera obscura of the childish brain.'*

Charles Baudelaire, 'The Philosophy of Toys'

*'For a sight will only survive in the queer
pool in which we deposit our memories if it has
the good luck to ally itself with some other
emotion by which it is preserved.'*

Virginia Woolf, 'The Sun and the Fish'

*You'll find no other lands, my friend,*
*speeding with sails unfurled.*

*Your city will go with you.*
*Through its streets and Squares.*

*You'll still be strolling,*
*as you strolled, despite your prayers.*

from 'The City' by C.P. Cavafy, translated by Hubert Butler

The quotes in this notebook are taken from the following titles,
all published by Notting Hill Editions.*

*Five Ways of Being a Painting and other essays*
The six winners of the £20,000 Notting Hill Editions Essay Prize,
featuring 'The Future of Nostalgia' by Patrick McGuinness.
Contributors include William Max Nelson, Laura Esther Wolfson,
Garret Keizer, Karen Holmberg and Dasha Shkurpela.

*I Remember*
by Joe Brainard
A cult classic. As autobiography, Brainard's method
was brilliantly simple: to set down specific memories as they
rose to the surface of his consciousness.

*On Dolls*
Edited by Kenneth Gross
The essays in this collection explore the seriousness of play
and the mysteries of inanimate life. Includes contributions
from Baudelaire, Rilke, Kafka and Freud.

*Essays on the Self*
by Virginia Woolf. Introduced by Joanna Kavenna.
In these essays Virginia Woolf explores the nature of the finite self,
and how individual experience might be relayed.

*The Invader Wore Slippers*
by Hubert Butler. Introduced by John Banville.
John Banville introduces a selection of Butler's
masterful essays on Europe.

*All titles are available in the UK and some titles are available
in the rest of the world. A selection of our titles is distributed in the
US and Canada by New York Review Books. For more information
on available titles, please visit www.nyrb.com.